## 344 VICTIMS OF PRETORIA PIT – SOME FACTS

**1: OPENED** - The shafts were sunk in 1900-01

**2: OFFICIAL NAME:** The Official name of the pit (or Colliery) was Hulton Colliery Bank Pits No's 3 & 4.

**3: POPULAR NAME:** The popular name was PRETORIA – because the shafts were sunk at the same time as, during the Anglo Boer War, the British captured the South African republic's capital city 'Pretoria' in June 1900

**4: PROPRIETORS:** Hulton Colliery Company. The General Manager of the Hulton Collieries was Alfred Joseph Tonge.

**5: DISASTER:** An explosion occurred at 7.50am on Wednesday 21st Dec 1910

**6: LOCATION OF THE DISASTER:** originating at the west end of North Plodder
No.2 coal face, under the fields north of Wood End Farm on the Hulton estates.

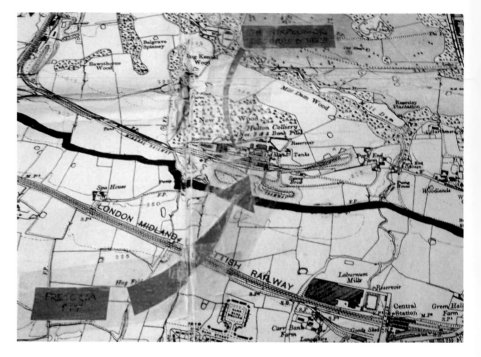

**7: COAL SEAMS:** =5 (known as 'mines' in this part of Lancashire).

**8: DEEPEST - ARLEY 'MINE':** at 1300ft (396m) worked from No.4 shaft.

**9: THREE QUARTERS 'MINE':** 1083ft (330m) worked from 3 & 4 shafts.

**10: YARD 'MINE':** 918ft (280m) worked from 3 & 4 shafts.

**11: PLODDER 'MINE'** 822ft (250m) worked from No.3 shaft.

**12: TRENCHERBONE 'MINE'** 438ft (134m) worked from No.4 shaft.

**13: CAUSE of EXPLOSION:** The official report into the disaster (Redmayne 1911) concluded that a damaged safety lamp ignited gas (methane/firedamp) pouring from an extensive roof fall

**14: DEATH TOLL:** The official total was 344 deaths, comprising 328 colliery employees, and 16 contractors and their staff

**15: SURVIVORS: 545** men were rescued from the No.4 pit (out of the Arley & Trencherbone Mines), some suffering from the effects of the gas. At least two from No.4 Pit, (J. Sharples and G. Partington), were badly gassed, and taken to Bolton Infirmary where they developed pneumonia, but recovered. John Sharples appeared on a postcard of the time as one of three Pretoria survivors. William Davenport and Joseph Staveley were the only survivors in No.3 Pit.

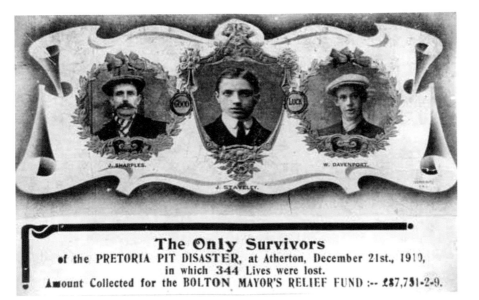

**The Only Survivors**
of the PRETORIA PIT DISASTER, at Atherton, December 21st., 1910, in which 344 Lives were lost.
Amount Collected for the BOLTON MAYOR'S RELIEF FUND :-- £87,731-2-9.

**16: BODIES RECOVERED:** Although the official death toll is 344, only 343 bodies were recovered, so only 343 deaths were ever registered. 327 deaths were registered in the name of a victim, and 16 deaths were registered as unknown males, each with an estimated age.

**17: 1ˢᵗ BODY TO BE RECOVERED: Richard Clayton, aged 52 on the 21ˢᵗ Dec.**

**18: 'ARLEY MINE':** **1** died Richard Clayton age 52. Cause of death: Suffocation

**19: 'THREE QUARTERS MINE': = 21** died in the Three Quarters Mine District, mostly from CO gas, though 7 of these were also burnt.

**20: 'YARD MINE' = 205 died** *(including Fountain Byers, aged 33,(picture on right) who was brought out alive, but died the next day in the Bolton Infirmary).*

**140** died in the Downbrow District, including 48 who were struggling back to the shafts along the East Level. Only 6 of the Downbrow victims were killed by explosive effects alone, whereas 105 died solely from CO gas poisoning, with no physical injuries. A further 20 killed by gas were also burnt

23 died in the East Jig District. 15 were killed solely by CO gas, the rest by some combination of gas and explosion. Only 2 were burnt.

42 died in the Top Yard District. Over half were killed by combined explosion and CO gassing, the rest from CO alone. 26% suffered burns, a similar proportion to the Three Quarters District, but much lower than in the Plodder Districts, some by a combination of gas and explosion. Only 2 were burnt.

**21: 'PLODDER MINE'= 95 died**

The explosion originated in the North Plodder District, and 61 died there. At the site of the explosion on North Plodder No.2 face, 17 of the 18 bodies showed explosion damage, and half were burnt. Only one man died solely from CO gassing.

34 died in the South Plodder District. 24 were killed by explosion, 13 directly while 11 survived long enough for CO gassing to contribute.

**22: PIT SHAFT AREA = 22 died**

The blast hit the shafts area with great force, hurling 7 bodies into No.3 shaft and one into No.4 shaft. 22 in total died in this area, all but 2 being killed by explosive violence (one was the under-manager, protected in his office from the blast, but not from gas).

**23: CAUSE OF DEATH BY VIOLENCE (EXPLOSION) = 9%**

**24: CAUSE OF DEATH BY GAS = 91%**

**25: LAST BODY TO BE RECOVERED:** Thomas Farrimond, aged 40, recovered on the 14th February 1911.

**Thomas Farrimond**

Photo above cropped from photograph of the Wingates Temperance Brass Band, when they were British Champions in 1906

**26: BODY STILL TO BE RECOVERED:** 6 Mar 1911 the BEN reported that *"Work is still being pushed forward for the recovery of the remaining body in the Pretoria pit, so far no trace of it has been found."* – no trace was ever found.

**27: UNIDENTIFIED DEAD:** 24 unidentified bodies were buried in a vault in Westhoughton Cemetery. Eight were later identified from clothing, property and photographs, but not reinterred. The remaining 16 deaths were registered as unknown males. The 17 whose deaths were not registered by name are:- Thomas Aldred age 14; James Baxter age 32; John Bullough age 55; William Connolly age 16; Robert Cowburn age 16; Leonard Emmett age 18; Thomas Faulkner age 16; Richard Goulding age 34; Edward Harris age 14; Robert Marsh age 20; John James Oakes age 13; James Pauldin age 21; Joseph Tyldesley age 17; Walter Vickers age 28; John Waring age 14; Fred Wolstencroft age 39; Arthur Woods age 14.

**The body of one of those named above was not recovered.**

**28: RESCUE:** *"I'm not forcing anyone to go down, we may come back and we may not, I'll be the first"*

- said Mr A.J. Tonge, the manager of Hulton Collieries, asking for a party of volunteers to go down the shaft.....eight men silently followed him.

When they reached the mine, they could not explore very far because the air was not yet clear. There was destruction everywhere.

The little rescue party, which included two young doctors, started to move as far as they could down the 'brow'...........

**29:VOLUNTEERS:** The eight men who volunteered to go with Mr Tonge were:

John Hardman
James Hartley
John Herring
John Hilton
William Markland
James Moss
James H. Polley
Robert Roberts

**30: DOCTORS:** The two doctors who accompanied them were:

Dr. John Cooper Russell
Dr. William Hamer Leigh

Howe Bridge Rescue Team
1910

# FACT 31:

# Rescuers & their Medals

| Ainsworth | J.H | B | Aldred | Joseph | B |
|---|---|---|---|---|---|
| Atherton | Frank | B | Atherton | H.Stanley | B |
| Barnes | E | B | Barnes | Walter | B |
| Bateson | Joshua | B | Beydell | J | B |
| Brown | P | B | Brown | P (Jnr) | B |
| Bryan | W | B | Bull | R.F. | B |
| Bullough | Edmund | B J R | Bullough | John | B J R |
| Butler | R | B | Byers | James | B |
| Chadwick | Thomas | B | Christenson | Joseph | B |
| Clarke | James | B | *Clayton* | *Edward* | *B* |
| Close | G. | B | Coe | W.H. | B |
| Corner | John | B | Corner | W. | B R |
| Cowgill? | W.H. | B | Crook | Gilbert | B |
| Croston | James | B | Croston | James | B |
| Cunliffe | J | B | Divine | J | B |
| Dixon | Gerrard W. | B R | Dixon | Harry Oliver | B J R |
| Drinnan | Lambert | B | Dyson | John W. | B |
| Eames | C.W | B | Ellis | J. | B |
| Ellison | J. | B | Evans | Isaac | B |
| Ewins | Walter | B | Ewins | William Alfred | B |
| Fairhurst | G (or J) | B | Fielding | J | B |
| Fielding | R | B | Fletcher | Clement | B |
| Fletcher | Leonard R. | B | Fletcher | Norman | B |
| Gerrard | John | B J R | Greenhalgh | Robert | B J R |
| Gregory | James | B | Grundy | D | B |
| Grundy | Thomas | B | Halliday | G (or C) | B R |
| Halliwell | Albert | B | Hardman | John | E B R |
| Harrison | A.R. | B | Hartley | James | E B J R |
| Herring | John | E B J R | Hill | W.H. (Sgt.Maj) | B |
| Hilton | John | E B J R | Hilton | John | B |
| Hindley | James | B | Horrocks | John | B J |
| Hughes | William | B | Hunt | J | B |
| Hyam | R | B | Janson | William H. | B |
| Job | William | B | Jobson | James | B |
| Kane | M | B | Kay | Richard | B |
| Knowles | John K. | B | Leech | Clive | B |
| Leigh, Dr. | Wm.Hamer | B J R | Leyland | John J. | B |
| Lindsay | James | B | Longmate | J. | B |
| Lowe | J. | B | Lyons | J. | B |
| Magnall | Benjamin | B J R | Magnall | Mark | B |
| Makin | H | B | Manley | H | B |

# 344 Victims of Pretoria Pit – Some Facts

| | | | | | |
|---|---|---|---|---|---|
| Markland | William | E B J R | Marsh | W. | B J R |
| Marsh | W | B J R | Martin | William | B |
| Millington | R. | B | Monks | J | B |
| Morris | A. | B | Morris | Benjamin | B |
| Moss | James | E B J R | Mottram | T.H. | B |
| Mullineaux | Adam | B | Mullineaux | J | B |
| Newton | C | B | Norris | W | B |
| Nutter | W | B | Orchard | A.J. | B |
| Ord | John | B | Owen | D | B |
| Owens | ? | B | Polley | James Henry | E B J R |
| Potter | William | B | Prince | S | B |
| Racker, Dr. | E. Clifford | B | Ramsden | Joseph | B |
| Ratcliffe | George | B | Rawson | Horace | B |
| Ridyard | George C. | B | Rigby | J | B |
| Roberts | Robert | E B J R | Robinson | John | B |
| Rosecamp | A.J. | B | Rushton | Arthur | B |
| Rushton | J.N. | B | Russell Dr. | John Cooper | B J R |
| Schofield | W. | B R | Scowcroft | Thomas | B |
| Sergeant | William | B | Shambley | Job | B |
| Shaw | J.T. | B | Sidlow | R | B |
| Singleton | N. | B | Singleton | W | B |
| Smith | F. | B | Smith | Henry (Harry) | B |
| Smith | William | B | Stayley | A. | B |
| Stott | Abraham | B J R | Sumner | R. | B |
| Thomas | J. | B | Thomas | Joseph | B |
| Thomasson | Joseph | B | Thompson | Ben | B |
| Thompson | Chris | B | Tonge | Alfred Joseph | E J*R*B |
| Tonge | James | B | Tonge | William | B |
| Topping | H | B | Turton | J | B R |
| Turton | William | B V | Twigg | Joseph | B |
| Walshaw | J | B | Williams | George | B |
| Williams | John | B J R | Williams | Llewellyn Edw. | E J B R |
| Williams | Richard | B | Williams | Thomas | B |
| Wilson | Charles | B | Wilson | George | B |
| Wilson | Leon | B | Winstanley | H.B. | B |
| Winstanley | James | B | Wolstencroft | W | B |
| Wood | P.L. | B | Wordsworth | W | B |
| Wallwork | Jesse | B | Wallwork | Robert | B |
| Warburton | S | B | Yates | J | B |

# SEE OVERLEAF FOR KEY TO RESCUERS' MEDALS…..

## KEY TO RESCUERS' MEDALS

## E = Edward Medal (mines) II Class, Bronze

Instituted in July 1907, size 33mm.

Description: (Obverse) the monarch's effigy; (reverse) a miner rescuing a stricken comrade, with the caption "For Courage" across the top.

Designed by W. Reynolds-Stephens, funded by a group of philanthropic individuals led by Mr A Hewlett, a leading mine owner.

Awarded for life saving in mines and quarries, in two grades: first class (Silver) and second class (Bronze). Medals were engraved with the names of the recipients, and since the 1930's, the date and place of the action were added.

Living recipients were invited to exchange their medals for the George Cross in 1971. The last awards to living recipients were made in 1949

**The Edward Medal (Mines). The example above is silver**

## 10 Pretoria Rescuers received the Bronze medal.

# J = LIFE SAVING MEDAL OF THE ORDER OF St. JOHN of JERUSALEM (Bronze).

# J* = LIFE SAVING MEDAL OF THE ORDER OF St. JOHN of JERUSALEM (Silver).

The Medal is circular and manufactured in bronze or silver, and is 37mm diameter.

Obverse: In the centre the eight pointed cross of the Order embellished with two lions and two unicorns in the interstices. Within a circular border with the words "FOR SERVICE IN THE CAUSE OF HUMANITY" in seriffed capitals.

Reverse: A sprig of St.John's wort bound with a ribbon bearing the words "JERUSALEM ENGLAND". Within a circular border the words AWARDED BY THE GRAND PRIORY OF THE ORDER OF THE HOSPITAL OF ST.JOHN OF JERUSALEM.

Ribbon: Watered black of one and one quarter inches suspended from a small ring.

Alfred Joseph Tonge was awarded the Silver medal, which is now in Bolton Museum (see left).

20 others were awarded the Bronze medal.

**R= ROYAL HUMANE SOCIETY MEDAL (Bronze)**

**R\* = ROYAL HUMANE SOCIETY MEDAL (Silver)**

**V =** *'In Memoriam' Vellum – awarded to Mrs William Turton, the widow of William Turton who was the only 'Rescuer' to die during the rescue operations in Pretoria.*

Alfred Joseph Tonge was awarded the Silver medal

25 Rescuers were awarded the Bronze Medal

Vellum posthumously awarded to William Turton.

# B = BOLTON & DISTRICT HUMANE SOCIETY MEDAL

There were 160 Bolton & District Humane Society medals awarded to the Rescuers.

This was specially designed to commemorate the actions of the rescuers on December 21st 1910 at the Pretoria Pit.

This was awarded posthumously to Edward Clayton

## HOWE BRIDGE RESCUE STATION – opened in 1908

### PHOTOGRAPH KINDLY SUPPLIED BY
### MRS BARBARA HAWORTH (nee Simkin)

Herbert     Jack Corbett     Sgt Major Hill

J. Pilkington    Peter Simkin    E.Holt    P.Seddon    R. Berry

Shortly after the opening of the rescue station at Howe Bridge, the first call was to assist at Maypole Colliery near Wigan, where 76 lives were lost. This was the first recorded use of breathing apparatus in Lancashire and one of the first in the country. At that time, there were only six trained men and a limited number of apparatus at the station. **Following the incident a special medal was struck by the coal owners and each of the six men was presented with one.**

**The second call came two years later, in 1910, to the Pretoria Pit at Westhoughton where 344 men and boys were killed in an explosion and there was evidence at that time of the considerably improved "Proto" apparatus. Again, a medal was struck and awarded to certain of the rescue men. This was the first time that several hundred rescue men took part in an operation, thus emphasising the tremendous progress which had been made in such a short time.**

**32: MOST FAMILY MEMBERS LOST:**

**Tyldesley family at Wingates** – Miriam (Hurst) Tyldesley lost her husband , four sons, and two brothers. She died in 1913. There is a memorial in Wingates Churchyard to the Tyldesley family.

**Houghton family from Chequerbent** — Mrs Annie Houghton lost her husband and three sons.

**33: OLDEST VICTIMS: Thomas Greenhalgh aged 61** (back fireman) was the oldest of the Pretoria victims. He had worked in the pits for some 50 years.

A Rescuer from Chequerbent Pits, **William Turton,** was 62 years old. The old miner died while helping to extinguish a small fire in the South Plodder District on the day of the explosion. The report of his burial service is headed "Funeral

of a Hero" (BEN 24 Dec 1910), for so he was regarded. But a later report about his death published at the time of the adjourned inquest proceedings, is headed "Death of a Rescuer. In Search of His Son" (BEN 27 Jan 1911). This account appears to have triggered unwarranted speculation that Turton died while desperately trying to find family members he believed trapped by the explosion, rather that following orders to make the pit safe. After considerable investigation into William Turton's death and any concern he showed about finding his son, was simply to establish the whereabouts of James, an experienced collier and fireman, who was elsewhere helping with exploration of the damaged pit. William Turton died, not in careless self-interest, but in trying to help a workmate put out a fire- a lethal hazard in a coal mine.

**34: YOUNGEST VICTIMS: all aged 13:**

**Fred**erick Stanley Houghton aged 13, birth registered 3$^{rd}$ Q 1897

**Jam**es Ernest Withington aged 13,  born 12 Jul 1897

**John** James Oakes aged 13,  born 26 February 1897

**Will**iam Green aged 13, birth registered 2$^{nd}$ Q 1897

**Jose**ph Morris who was aged 13, and would have been 14 on New Year's Day

**35: LADS AGED 14 Years old – there were seventeen of these.**

**36: LADS AGED 15 Years old – there were thirteen of these.**

**37: FIRST DAY DOWN PIT:**

**Fred**erick Stanley Houghton, aged 13, left school the week before.

**Anth**ony Doxey aged 18 – reported to be his first day down the pit.

**38:  MINING STUDENT FROM BIRKENHEAD:**

**Robert Curwen, aged 19,** was a mining student who had previously worked in Walker Bros. Foundry in Wigan.  He came from a wealthy family, his late father being a shipowner in Liverpool.  His parents were both dead.  He was buried in the very ornate & elaborate family grave in Flaybrick Cemetery, Birkenhead.

**39:  FATHER OF VICTIM DIED OF SHOCK:**

**William Connolly, aged 16,** of 25 Chorley Road, Wingates, was one of the victims whose body was never identified, thought to be buried in the vault for Unknown Victims.  His father (Patrick) had a weak heart, and died three days after the disaster, on December 24$^{th}$ – apparently from the shock. Patrick's body was buried in the Roman Catholic cemetery, which is opposite the Memorial to the Unknown Victims.

## 40: COLDSTREAM GUARDSMAN WAS ONE OF THE VICTIMS:

**William Dyke, a collier aged 39,** of 4, Manchester Road, Higher Ince, Wigan, lodged in Sloan Street, Daubhill. His body was brought to the surface late on the Friday night 13th January 1911.

He was an ex-soldier, and served for 7 years in the Coldstream Guards. He was called up with the reserves during the South African war, and took part in the fighting at Modder River. Dyke was injured in his right arm by a bullet, and was invalided home. Through the injury, he was granted a larger pension. He had worked in the employ of the colliery for several years. He was a well-built man.

A brother of the deceased had been to the colliery every day since the explosion in search of his brother, and when the body was found, he identified it. Looking for his grave in 2007 – Wigan cemetery office said that the unused space in the grave had been bought by another family....therefore William Dyke had no memorial stone.

William Dyke had dependants – his father aged 64, his mother aged 62, his brother Charles aged 41, who was blind and deaf, and his brother Israel, aged 26, who was a cripple. The family all lived at Higher Ince.

## 41: WIDOW ANXIOUS TO PAY HUSBAND'S DEBTS:

**David Grundy, a collier aged 48** from Little Hulton. David and Fanny Grundy had no children at the time of the disaster, yet they had had 5 children from 1885 to 1898, and all were infant deaths.

In a WCA (Workman's Compensation Act) hearing it was reported: "In the first case, that of Fanny Grundy, Mr Horridge, who appeared for her, said that at one time the deceased was in a coal-bagging business, but he went bankrupt, and at the time of his death he was owing £43 to the Ellesmere Collieries for coal, and £90 which he had received as a trustee for the children of a relative." His Honour said the woman was not liable for these debts, and he did not know why they should be paid out of the compensation. He asked if she had any children. Mr Horridge: "No Sir". His Honour: "What has she to live on?" Mr

Horridge: "She would have to work – she is very anxious that these children should be paid" His Honour said the widow could pay the Ellesmere Colliery out of the money she had, and he would order that the children should be paid their share of the £90 out of the fund as they came of age. (BJG 24 Feb 1911).

**42: 'LITTLE' BILLY NAYLOR , aged 15,** was reported to be a good chorister who

earned coins singing for the men while down the pit.

There is a recording of his sister Agnes talking about him on *'Pretoria Remembered'* in the North West Sound Archive at Clitheroe, Lancs.

The family lived at 15 Waters Nook, Westhoughton, and Billy was employed as a "Lasher-on", which is a haulage hand whose job was to lash a tub chain to a haulage rope.

**43: MUSICIANS: -**

**Enoch Arthur Bates, aged 23,** was a member of Daubhill Salvation Army Barracks, and played euphonium in the band. It was said that he played many instruments. He was born in Garston, near Liverpool, and his parents and sister were also members of the Salvation Army. Indeed, the family was at the Pretoria Pit on the fateful day of the explosion, attending to the needs of the bereaved families, even though they, themselves, were also bereaved. They are photographed (below) with the mortuary attendants, and with Rev. Father Adolphus L. Coelenbier of the Sacred Heart Church.

**John Hodson, aged 35,** was a trombonist in Westhoughton Old Prize Band.

**Edward Thomas, aged 27,** was an accomplished Violinist.

EDWARD THOMAS,
489, Manchester-road, Westhoughton. A most accomplished violinist, who had been studying hard and intended making his way to the front on the concert platform.

## MEMBERS OF WINGATES TEMPERANCE BAND WHO PERISHED IN PRETORIA

Thomas Farrimond aged 40

Samuel Farrimond aged 37

William Cowburn aged 40

John Bullough aged 55

Albert Lonsdale aged 37

Fountain Byers aged 33

Edward Halliwell Green aged 22

## 44: SPORTSMEN WHO WERE AMONGST THE DEAD –

**SWIMMING:** Joseph Darlington, aged 28 – was a member of Tyldesley Swimming Club, captained Atherton Water Polo Team, and also played for Manchester League.

**BOWLING:**   John Higson, aged 43, a local bowler.

Richard Mather, aged 49 – a bowler at Red Lion Inn.

Sam Woodward, aged 34 – bowler, nicknamed "Pot Cat"

Mark Critchley, (below) aged 22, was a notable bowler.

**WRESTLING:**

Albert Shambley, aged 17                    William Shambley, aged 28

Two more wrestlers were:-

**Joe Topping, aged 23,**who was a competition wrestler who toured the country.

**Matthew Seddon, aged 24,** was also a well-known wrestler.

## HARRIERS:

Six members of Chequerbent Harriers were:-

**William Lees Ascroft, aged 14**

**Gerald Hastie, aged 19**

**Thomas Hastie aged 21**

**Edward Houseman (or Outram), aged 15**

**James Leigh, aged 14**

**Thomas Worthington, aged 36**

## CYCLING:

**William Southern, aged 29** - a member of Westhoughton Cycling Club, and also the caretaker of Trinity Wesleyan Church.

## CRICKET:

**Thomas Henry Coop, aged 28-** conveyor attendant, was a player in the Bolton & District Cricket Association.

Other players in the Bolton & District Cricket Association were:-

**James Hodgkiss, aged 31** – Collier, of Chequerbent

**Lewis Hodgkiss, aged 39** – Fireman, of Chequerbent… n.b: his watch, which had been stopped by the force of the blast was later used in the public inquiry to establish the time of the explosion (newspaper report).

**Abel Mangnall, aged 24** –Collier, of Wingates

**William Ratcliffe, aged 31** –Collier, of Bolton Road, Westhoughton

**William Turton, aged 62** – Fireman from the Chequerbent pit.

**John Austin, aged 37 –** Collier, of Chequerbent

**John Lawrence Coffey, aged 28** – Collier, of Wingates

**Thomas Laughna, aged 23** – Collier, of Wigan Road, Deane

## 45:   MORE PHOTOGRAPHS OF PRETORIA VICTIMS……

**Thomas Aldred,  aged 14 ,** Haulage Hand

**William Ashton, aged 22,** Collier

**Arthur Aspden, aged 21,** Drawer

**John Thomas Aspden ,aged 37,** Collier

**John Baxter, aged 30,** Collier

**John Baxter, aged 58,** Collier

**Sam Baxter, aged 24,** Collier

**Israel Bennett, aged 24,** Collier

**Thomas Bennett, aged 22,** Collier

**George Boardman, aged 23,** Conveyor Attendant

**Thomas Alfred Calderbank, aged 23,** Collier

**William Connolly, aged 16,** Dataller

**William Cowburn, aged 42,** Collier **(Chairman of Wingates Temperance Band)**

**Sydney Delafield, aged 25,** Collier

**Thomas Delafield, aged 23,** Collier

**Thomas Dunn, aged 34,** Collier

**Leonard Emmett, aged 18,** Drawer

**James Farrimond, aged 15,** Haulage Hand

**Joseph Greenall, aged 34,** Collier

**Thomas Greenall, aged 37,** Collier

**Edward Harris, aged 15,** Lasher On

**Gerald Hastie, aged 19,** Conveyor Attendant

**Thomas Hastie, aged 21,** Conveyor Attendant (in Territorial Army Uniform).

**James Higham, aged 59,** Haulage Engineman

**James Hilton, aged 25,** Collier

**Montague Boardman Hilton, aged 29,** Dataller

**William Hilton,** aged 26, Drawer

**James Holden, aged 15,** Haulage Hand

**John Hosker aged 16** Dataller

**Albert Howarth, aged 16,** Haulage Hand

**Stephen Hulme, aged 24,** Collier

**Thomas Hurst, aged 19,** Drawer

**Joseph Jones, aged 24,** Drawer

**Albert Lonsdale, aged 37,** Collier **(Secretary & Cornet player of Wingates Temperance Brass Band).**

**James Lovett, aged 28,**Collier

**Joseph Lovett, aged 50,** Dataller

**Wright Lovett, aged 16,** Lasher-on

**Daniel Mather, age 23,** Collier

**William Meads, age 49,** Collier

**Thomas Wilcock Molyneux, aged 26,** Collier

**James Partington ,aged 43,** Collier

**Thomas Partington, aged 19,** Collier

**Herbert Prescott, aged 24,** Drawer

**John Prescott, aged 23,** Drawer

**William Ratcliffe, aged 31,** Collier

**John Roberts, aged 26,** Collier

**Mark Skeldon, aged 28,** Collier

**William Southern, aged 29,** Collier

**Paul Thomasson, aged 45,** Collier

**Richard Thomasson ,aged 51,** Collier

Date on back Jan 1909 J. Tyldesley **John Tyldesley Jnr., aged 25,** Collier

**Albert Unsworth aged 17** Lasher On

**James Unsworth, aged 30,** Collier

**John Waring, aged 14,** Lasher on

**John Wild, aged 17,** Dataller

**Richard Wild, aged 45,** Dataller

**Thomas Wild, aged 15,** Dataller

**Alfred Edward Woods, aged 15,** Haulage Hand

**James Worthington, aged 59,** Collier

**Henry (Harry) Wyper, aged 21,** Collier

**The photographs shown are just a fraction of the 344 men & boys who perished in the PRETORIA pit disaster, 21st December 1910.**

# "MAY THEY ALL REST IN PEACE"

Pam Clarke for  Westhoughton Local History Group

## Full List of the victims of the Pretoria Pit disaster, 21st December 1910

| | | | |
|---|---|---|---|
| Thomas Aldred | age 14 | Haulage Hand | born: Atherton |
| William Anderton | age 15 | Haulage Hand | born: Westhoughton |
| William Lees Ascroft | age 14 | Haulage Hand | born: Westhoughton |
| William Ashton | age 22 | Collier | born: Wigan |
| Arthur Aspden | age 21 | Collier | born: Westhoughton |
| John Thomas Aspden | age 37 | Collier | born: Westhoughton |
| Walter Aspden | age 28 | Drawer | born: Westhoughton |
| Joseph Edward Atherton | age 14 | Haulage Hand | born: Westhoughton |
| John Austin | age 37 | Collier | born: Sheffield, Yorks |
| James Baker | age 25 | Collier | born: Golden Hill, Staffs |
| Fred Balforn | age 30 | Drawer | born: Westhoughton |
| Job Ball | age 52 | Dataller | born: Rumworth |
| Enoch Arthur Bates | age 23 | Drawer | born: Garston, West Derby |
| Joseph Grundy Battersby | age 16 | Haulage Hand | born: Westhoughton |
| James Baxter | age 32 | Dataller | born: Astley |
| John Baxter | age 30 | Collier | born: Astley |
| John Baxter | age 57 | Collier | born: Astley |
| Samuel Baxter | age 24 | Collier | born: Astley |
| William Bellew | age 19 | Drawer | born: Preston |
| Henry Bennett | age 20 | Drawer | born: Westhoughton |
| Israel Bennett | age 23 | Collier | born: Westhoughton |
| Thomas Bennett | age 22 | Collier | born: Westhoughton |
| William Bennett | age 17 | Drawer | born: Westhoughton |
| James Berry | age 21 | Engineers Fitter | born: Aspull |
| Henry Blundell | age 38 | Collier | born: Westhoughton |
| George Boardman | age 23 | Conv.Attendt. | born: Westhoughton |
| John Boardman | age 33 | Collier | born: Westhoughton |
| Walter Boardman | age 28 | Collier | born: Westhoughton |
| William Alfred Bond | age 28 | Collier | born: Westhoughton |
| John Bradley | age 20 | Drawer | born: Westhoughton |
| William Bradley | age 50 | Collier | born: Westhoughton |
| William Bromby | age 37 | Collier | born: Lincolnshire |
| William Thomas Brown | age 39 | Collier | born: Westhoughton |
| Adam Bullough | age 28 | Collier | born: Westhoughton |
| John Bullough | age 55 | Collier | born: Westhoughton |
| Fountain Byers | age 33 | Pusher-on | born: Adlington |
| Alfred Calderbank | age 48 | Back Fireman | born: Westhoughton |
| Robert Calderbank | age 23 | Dataller | born: Westhoughton |
| Thomas Alfred Calderbank | age 23 | Collier | born: Westhoughton |
| William Calderbank | age 21 | Drawer | born: Westhoughton |
| Cyril Cattell | age 14 | Haulage Hand | born: Warrington |
| William Catterall | age 40 | Collier | born: Buckley, Flintshire |

344 Victims of Pretoria Pit – Some Facts

| | | | |
|---|---|---|---|
| Jesse Chadwick | age 23 | Collier | born: Middle Hulton |
| Orlando Chadwick | age 42 | Collier | born: Westhoughton |
| Arthur Chetwynd | age 21 | Drawer | born: Stalybridge, Cheshire |
| James Clarke | age 24 | Collier | born: Northwich, Cheshire |
| Richard Clayton | age 52 | Fireman | born: Congleton, Cheshire |
| Edward Clynes | age 15 | Lasher-on | born: Atherton |
| Ambrose Coffey | age 24 | Collier | born: Walkden |
| Frederick Coffey | age 30 | Collier | born: Walkden |
| John Lawrence Coffey | age 28 | Collier | born: Walkden |
| William Connolly | age 16 | Dataller | born: Westhoughton |
| Thomas Henry Coop | age 28 | Conv.Attendt. | born: Westhoughton |
| Robert Cope | age 19 | Haulage Hand | born: Atherton |
| Robert Cowburn | age 16 | Haulage Hand | born: Westhoughton |
| Samuel Cowburn | age 55 | Collier | born: Westhoughton |
| William Cowburn | age 40 | Collier | born: Westhoughton |
| Mark Critchley | age 22 | Hooker-on | born: Westhoughton |
| Samuel Critchley | age 29 | Collier | born: Westhoughton |
| Walter Crook | age 16 | Haulage Hand | born: Atherton |
| Ralph Croston | age 25 | Drawer | born: Westhoughton |
| William Croston | age 38 | Collier | born: Hindley |
| Robert Clifford Curwen | age 19 | Student-Mining | born: Birkenhead, Cheshire |
| Joseph Darlington | age 28 | Collier | born: Tyldesley |
| Benjamin Aaron Davies | age 23 | Collier | born: Bersham, Denbighshire |
| William Dawson | age 47 | Dataller | born: North Meols, Southport |
| Sydney Delafield | age 25 | Collier | born: Nether Silton, Yorkshire |
| Thomas Delafield | age 23 | Collier | born: Nether Silton, Yorkshire |
| Fred Dootson | age 27 | Collier | born: Westhoughton |
| Henry Dootson | age 24 | Drawer | born: Westhoughton |
| John Thomas Dootson | age 26 | Collier | born: Westhoughton |
| Samuel Dootson | age 30 | Collier | born: Westhoughton |
| Dennis Dorcey | age 14 | Lasher-on | born: Oldham |
| Anthony Doxey | age 18 | Drawer | born: Westhoughton |
| Harry Doxey | age 23 | Drawer | born: Westhoughton |
| Samuel Doxey | age 25 | Collier | born: Westhoughton |
| William Doxey | age 51 | Timberman | born: Westhoughton |
| Peter Duffy | age 25 | Pit Worker | born: Bolton |
| Thomas Dunn | age 34 | Collier | born: Manchester |
| William Dyke | age 39 | Collier | born: Wigan |
| James Eccleston | age 31 | Collier | born: Hindley Green |
| James Eccleston | age 60 | Collier | born: Bolton |
| William Eccleston | age 20 | Drawer | born: Hindley Green |
| Leonard Emmett | age 18 | Drawer | born: Westhoughton |
| Thomas Emmett | age 31 | Dataller | born: Harlington, Middx |
| Roland Evans | age 32 | Tunneller | born: Silverdale, Staffs |

| | | | |
|---|---|---|---|
| William Evans | age 26 | Collier | born: Ince-in-Makerfield |
| Richard Fairhurst | age 47 | Collier | born: Halliwell, Bolton |
| James Farrimond | age 15 | Haulage Hand | born: Westhoughton |
| Samuel Farrimond | age 37 | Collier | born: Rainford |
| Thomas Farrimond | age 40 | Collier | born: Rainford |
| Thomas Faulkner | age 16 | Haulage Hand | born: Sutton |
| Thomas Charles Faulkner | age 25 | Drawer | born: Kirkham |
| James Feely | age 31 | Dataller | born: Ireland |
| John Flood | age 27 | Drawer | born: Manchester |
| Walter Foster | age 28 | Conv.Attendt. | born: Hindley |
| Orlando Gerrard | age 21 | Fitter | born: Westhoughton |
| Thomas Gibbs | age 26 | Drawer | born: Holywell, Flintshire |
| Herbert Gibson | age 18 | Drawer | born: Westhoughton |
| Simeon Gibson | age 16 | Lasher-on | born: Westhoughton |
| Thomas Gill | age 22 | Drawer | born: Westhoughton |
| William Gore | age 42 | Collier | born: Standish |
| Richard Goulding | age 34 | Collier | born: Aspull |
| William Goulding | age 35 | Collier | born: Aspull |
| Edward Halliwell Green | age 22 | Drawer | born: Westhoughton |
| James Green | age 34 | Collier | born: Westhoughton |
| Peter Green | age 41 | Collier | born: Westhoughton |
| Richard Green | age 53 | Collier | born: Westhoughton |
| Thomas Green | age 28 | Collier | born: Westhoughton |
| William Green | age 31 | Lasher-on | born: Bolton |
| Joseph Greenall | age 34 | Collier | born: Thatto Heath, St Helens |
| Thomas Greenall | age 36 | Collier | born: Thatto Heath, St Helens |
| Thomas Greenhalgh | age 61 | Back Fireman | born: Westhoughton |
| Thomas Greenhalgh | age 24 | Collier | born: Westhoughton |
| Albert Griffiths | age 27 | Collier | born: Wolverhampton, Staffs |
| David Grundy | age 48 | Collier | born: Little Hulton |
| Albert Hardman | age 17 | Conv.Attendt. | born: Westhoughton |
| Samuel Hardman | age 19 | Drawer | born: Westhoughton |
| John Robert Hargreaves | age 27 | Drawer | born: Bolton |
| Edward Harris | age 14 | Lasher-on | born: Westhoughton |
| Nicholas Hartley | age 44 | Collier | born: Westhoughton |
| Gerald Hastie | age 19 | Conv.Attendt. | born: Northwich, Cheshire |
| Thomas Hastie | age 21 | Conv.Attendt. | born: Northwich, Cheshire |
| Frederick Hayes | age 43 | Collier | born: Westhoughton |
| William Hayes | age 28 | Collier | born: Westhoughton |
| Edward Haynes | age 35 | Drawer | born: Daubhill, Bolton |
| William Hesketh | age 26 | Conv.Attendt. | born: Westhoughton |
| John Edward E. Hewitt | age 45 | Electrician | born: Whitley, Cheshire |
| James Higham | age 60 | Hlge.Engineman | born: Atherton |
| Joseph Higham | age 23 | Drawer | born: Westhoughton |

| | | | |
|---|---|---|---|
| John Higson | age 44 | Collier | born: Rumworth |
| Peter Higson | age 46 | Dataller | born: Rumworth |
| William Higson | age 23 | Dataller | born: Deane, Bolton |
| James Hilton | age 25 | Collier | born: Westhoughton |
| Joseph Hilton | age 54 | Collier | born: Middle Hulton |
| Montague Boardman Hilton | age 29 | Dataller | born: Westhoughton |
| Percy Hilton | age 25 | Dataller | born: Westhoughton |
| William Hilton | age 26 | Drawer | born: Middle Hulton |
| Fred Hindle | age 22 | Dataller | born: Atherton |
| James Hodgkiss | age 31 | Collier | born: Farnworth |
| Lewis Hodgkiss | age 15 | Haulage Hand | born: Farnworth |
| Lewis Hodgkiss | age 39 | Fireman | born: Ince-in-Makerfield |
| Stanley Hodgkiss | age 14 | Haulage Hand | born: Westhoughton |
| John Hodson | age 35 | Collier | born: Westhoughton |
| James Edward Hogan | age 15 | Haulage Hand | born: Atherton |
| Henry Holden | age 31 | Collier | born: Westhoughton |
| James Holden | age 15 | Haulage Hand | born: Westhoughton |
| Edward Hollingsworth | age 33 | Collier | born: Westhoughton |
| William Hollingsworth | age 31 | Collier | born: Westhoughton |
| Albert Holt | age 28 | Collier | born: Middle Hulton |
| Frederick Hook | age 14 | Lasher-on | born: Atherton |
| Thomas Hope | age 15 | Haulage Hand | born: Pendlebury |
| Joseph Horrocks | age 19 | Conv.Attendt. | born: Westhoughton |
| Thomas Horrocks | age 49 | Collier | born: Rumworth |
| John Hosker | age 16 | Dataller | born: Leigh |
| Elias Houghton | age 23 | Collier | born: Horwich |
| Frederick Stanley Houghton | age 13 | Haulage Hand | born: Westhoughton |
| John Houghton | age 46 | Collier | born: Eccleston |
| John Thomas Houghton | age 46 | Collier | born: Wigan |
| Thomas Houghton | age 17 | Drawer | born: Westhoughton |
| Edward Houseman | age 15 | Haulage Hand | born: St Helens |
| Albert Howarth | age 16 | Haulage Hand | born: Westhoughton |
| Thomas Howcroft | age 34 | Collier | born: Rumworth |
| Thomas Howcroft | age 25 | Collier | born: Bolton |
| Stephen Hulme | age 29 | Collier | born: Blackrod |
| John Hundy | age 53 | Head Fireman | born: Brierley Hill, Staffs |
| Samuel Hundy | age 39 | Back Fireman | born: Brierley Hill, Staffs |
| James Hurst | age 50 | Collier | born: Westhoughton |
| Thomas Hurst | age 55 | Collier | born: Westhoughton |
| Thomas Hurst | age 19 | Drawer | born: Bolton |
| Thomas Hurst | age 49 | Collier | born: Liverpool |
| Richard Jolley | age 24 | Collier | born: Westhoughton |
| Thomas Jolley | age 49 | Collier | born: Blackrod |
| William Thompson Jolly | age 25 | Collier | born: Crook |

|  |  |  |  |
|---|---|---|---|
| Joseph Jones | age 24 | Drawer | born: Flintshire |
| William Kay | age 30 | Collier | born: Westhoughton |
| Edward Kenwright | age 28 | Collier | born: Holywell, Flintshire |
| Thomas Laughna | age 23 | Collier | born: Westhoughton |
| Frederick Lee | age 36 | Collier | born: Westhoughton |
| Josiah Lee | age 23 | Drawer | born: Tipton, Staffordshire |
| James Leigh | age 14 | Lasher-on | born: Westhoughton |
| John Leigh | age 42 | Collier | born: Westhoughton |
| Peter Leigh | age 50 | Collier | born: Westhoughton |
| Walter Leigh | age 21 | Drawer | born: Westhoughton |
| Joseph Leyland | age 24 | Collier | born: St Helens |
| Richard Light | age 45 | Collier | born: Wolverhampton, Staffs |
| James Livesey | age 17 | Drawer | born: Westhoughton |
| John Livesey | age 15 | Haulage Hand | born: Westhoughton |
| Richard Nelson Longmate | age 29 | Collier | born: Kearsley |
| Peter Longworth | age 23 | Collier | born: Middle Hulton |
| Albert Lonsdale | age 37 | Collier | born: Turton |
| James Lovett | age 28 | Collier | born: Westhoughton |
| Joseph Lovett | age 50 | Dataller | born: Westhoughton |
| Wright Lovett | age 16 | Lasher-on | born: Westhoughton |
| Andrew Lowe | age 23 | Drawer | born: Westhoughton |
| Abel Mangnall | age 22 | Collier | born: Westhoughton |
| Walter Mangnall | age 30 | Collier | born: Westhoughton |
| William E. G. Markland | age 17 | Conv. Attendt. | born: Westhoughton |
| Martin Marrin | age 30 | Collier | born: Westhoughton |
| Robert Marsh | age 20 | Drawer | born: Westhoughton |
| Thomas Marsh | age 55 | Collier | born: Westhoughton |
| Thomas Martin | age 23 | Dataller | born: Westhoughton |
| Daniel Mather | age 23 | Collier | born: Westhoughton |
| Edward Mather | age 35 | Collier | born: Aspull |
| Richard Mather | age 49 | Collier | born: Birkenhead, Cheshire |
| Joseph McCabe | age 22 | Drawer | born: Westhoughton |
| Matthew McCabe | age 24 | Drawer | born: Rainford |
| Michael McCabe | age 19 | Drawer | born: Hindley |
| James McDonald | age 26 | Collier | born: Neston, Cheshire |
| William Mead | age 49 | Collier | born: Liverpool |
| William H. Middlehurst | age 48 | Collier | born: Stourbridge, Staffs |
| Harry Miller | age 32 | Collier | born: Bolton |
| James Miller | age 28 | Collier | born: Westhoughton |
| Joseph Miller | age 30 | Collier | born: Westhoughton |
| James Mills | age 26 | Drawer | born: Earlstown |
| Michael Molloy | age 26 | Dataller | born: Ireland |
| Thomas Wilcock Molyneux | age 26 | Collier | born: St Helens |
| John Monks | age 19 | Drawer | born: Westhoughton |

# 344 Victims of Pretoria Pit – Some Facts

| | | | |
|---|---|---|---|
| Percival Monks | age 36 | Collier | born: Aspull |
| James Morris | age 30 | Collier | born: Bolton |
| John Morris | age 22 | Haulage Hand | born: Westhoughton |
| John Morris | age 36 | Collier | born: Coppull |
| Joseph Morris | age 13 | Lasher-on | born: Westhoughton |
| Robert Morris | age 43 | Collier | born: Coppull |
| William Morris | age 34 | Collier | born: Bolton |
| Peter Moss | age 15 | Haulage Hand | born: Atherton |
| William Edward Naylor | age 15 | Lasher-on | born: Westhoughton |
| Albert Norman | age 36 | Collier | born: Burslem, Staffordshire |
| David Nuttall | age 23 | Collier | born: Westhoughton |
| John James Oakes | age 13 | Lasher-on | born: Bolton |
| Thomas Owens | age 27 | Collier | born: Westhoughton |
| John Parr | age 51 | Collier | born: Wrightington |
| Harry Partington | age 19 | Drawer | born: Westhoughton |
| James Partington | age 42 | Collier | born: Middle Hulton |
| Joseph Partington | age 25 | Collier | born: Westhoughton |
| Samuel Partington | age 16 | Lasher-on | born: Atherton |
| Thomas Partington | age 24 | Collier | born: Westhoughton |
| Thomas Partington | age 19 | Collier | born: Westhoughton |
| William Partington | age 40 | Hooker-on | born: Westhoughton |
| James Pauldin | age 21 | Collier | born: Bolton |
| Enoch Pemberton | age 29 | Collier | born: Stalybridge, Cheshire |
| Fred Pemberton | age 16 | Lasher-on | born: Westhoughton |
| John Lowden Pemberton | age 21 | Drawer | born: Stalybridge, Cheshire |
| Harold Pendlebury | age 16 | Haulage Hand | born: Westhoughton |
| George Henry Perks | age 19 | Drawer | born: Westhoughton |
| George Percy Potter | age 16 | Drawer | born: Aspull |
| James Potter | age 15 | Haulage Hand | born: Aspull |
| William Potter | age 39 | Collier | born: Aspull |
| Herbert Prescott | age 24 | Drawer | born: Blackburn |
| John Prescott | age 23 | Drawer | born: Blackburn |
| Henry Price | age 22 | Collier | born: Bolton |
| James Price | age 42 | Collier | born: Ireland |
| Fred Ratcliffe | age 21 | Drawer | born: Westhoughton |
| Isaac Ratcliffe | age 23 | Night Fireman | born: Adlington |
| Thomas Ratcliffe | age 40 | Collier | born: Westhoughton |
| William Ratcliffe | age 31 | Collier | born: Westhoughton |
| Benjamin Riding | age 19 | Drawer | born: Westhoughton |
| Willie Riding | age 22 | Collier | born: Westhoughton |
| William Rigby | age 60 | Collier | born: Hindley |
| Albert Roberts | age 15 | Lasher-on | born: Westhoughton |
| John Roberts | age 27 | Collier | born: Buckley, Flintshire |
| Robert Roberts | age 21 | Collier | born: Westhoughton |

|  |  |  |  |
|---|---|---|---|
| Edward Rushton | age 36 | Undermanager | born: Walkden |
| John Rushton | age 31 | Collier | born: Walkden |
| George Sargeant | age 28 | Collier | born: Hindley |
| Edward Saunders | age 18 | Haulage Hand | born: Atherton |
| John Saunders | age 13 | Lasher-on | born: Atherton |
| Fred Schofield | age 20 | Collier | born: Horwich |
| James Schofield | age 35 | Collier | born: Barnsley, Yorkshire |
| William Schofield | age 32 | Collier | born: Horwich |
| Joseph Scoble | age 53 | Dataller | born: Landore, Swansea |
| James Seddon | age 22 | Collier | born: Westhoughton |
| James Seddon | age 22 | Collier | born: Westhoughton |
| John Wilfred Seddon | age 19 | Drawer | born: Westhoughton |
| Joseph Seddon | age 18 | Drawer | born: Bolton |
| Matthew Seddon | age 24 | Collier | born: Bolton |
| Matthew Seddon | age 50 | Collier | born: Westhoughton |
| Richard Seddon | age 24 | Dataller | born: Westhoughton |
| Albert Shambley | age 17 | Drawer | born: Westhoughton |
| William Shambley | age 28 | Collier | born: Westhoughton |
| George Sharples | age 60 | Collier | born: Over Darwen |
| Richard Sharples | age 33 | Collier | born: Rumworth |
| Ralph Shaw | age 35 | Collier | born: Lostock |
| Daniel Simmons | age 21 | Drawer | born: Westhoughton |
| Mark Skeldon | age 28 | Collier | born: Pendlebury |
| Albert Smith | age 25 | Collier | born: Pendlebury |
| Isaac Smith | age 30 | Drawer | born: Wigan |
| John Smith | age 43 | Dataller | born: Lostock |
| Thomas Smith | age 53 | Collier | born: Westhoughton |
| William Smith | age 46 | Collier | born: Westhoughton |
| Oliver Southern | age 21 | Drawer | born: Westhoughton |
| William Southern | age 29 | Collier | born: Westhoughton |
| Fred Southworth | age 22 | Collier | born: Bolton |
| Richard Lawrence Spencer | age 27 | Drawer | born: Westhoughton |
| Fred Teasdale | age 46 | Collier | born: Tryddyn, Flintshire |
| Daniel Thomas | age 35 | Collier | born: Wigan |
| Edward Thomas | age 26 | Collier | born: Ince, Wigan |
| William James Thomas | age 28 | Fireman | born: Ince, Wigan |
| Paul Thomasson | age 43 | Collier | born: Rumworth |
| Richard Thomasson | age 51 | Collier | born: Rumworth |
| Samuel Thornley | age 25 | Collier | born: Westhoughton |
| Richard Tonge | age 14 | Haulage Hand | born: Westhoughton |
| John Topping | age 53 | Collier | born: Little Hulton |
| Joseph Topping | age 23 | Collier | born: Walkden |
| John Edward Tumblety | age 20 | Dataller | born: Hindley |
| George Tunstall | age 56 | Collier | born: Cobridge, Staffordshire |

| | | | |
|---|---|---|---|
| George Tunstall | age 16 | Haulage Hand | born: Aspull |
| Moses Turner | age 21 | Haulage Hand | born: Hindley |
| William Turton | age 62 | Fireman (Chq.Pit) | born: Wigan |
| John Tyldesley | age 53 | Collier | born: Sutton |
| John Tyldesley | age 25 | Collier | born: Westhoughton |
| Joseph Tyldesley | age 17 | Drawer | born: Westhoughton |
| Thomas Hurst Tyldesley | age 23 | Drawer | born: Westhoughton |
| William Tyldesley | age 28 | Collier | born: Westhoughton |
| James Tyrer | age 48 | Collier | born: Westhoughton |
| Albert Unsworth | age 17 | Haulage Hand | born: Middle Hulton |
| James Unsworth | age 30 | Collier | born: Deane, Bolton |
| Jehu Unsworth | age 43 | Collier | born: Westhoughton |
| William Unsworth | age 23 | Drawer | born: Westhoughton |
| Herbert Vickers | age 22 | Drawer | born: Westhoughton |
| Walter Vickers | age 30 | Collier | born: Bolton |
| John Waring | age 14 | Lasher-on | born: Westhoughton |
| Samuel Wharmby | age 26 | Drawer | born: Little Hulton |
| Charles Wharton | age 36 | Collier | born: Rumworth |
| Benjamin While | age 20 | Collier | born: Rowley Regis, Staffs |
| Robert Whittaker | age 32 | Collier | born: Darwen |
| William Wignall | age 14 | Lasher-on | born: Westhoughton |
| John Wild | age 17 | Dataller | born: Bolton |
| Richard Wild | age 44 | Dataller | born: Darwen |
| Thomas Wild | age 15 | Dataller | born: Bolton |
| George Williams | age 24 | Drawer | born: Atherton |
| John Andrew Wise | age 44 | Collier | born: Bootle |
| James Ernest Withington | age 13 | Haulage Hand | born: Westhoughton |
| Fred Wolstencroft | age 39 | Collier | born: Bolton |
| Alfred Edward Woods | age 15 | Haulage Hand | born: Lostock |
| Arthur Woods | age 14 | Lasher-on | born: Westhoughton |
| Percy Woodward | age 18 | Dataller | born: Westhoughton |
| Samuel Woodward | age 34 | Collier | born: Westhoughton |
| Thomas Woodward | age 32 | Drawer | born: Westhoughton |
| Walter Woodward | age 41 | Carpenter | born: Westhoughton |
| James Worthington | age 59 | Collier | born: Middle Hulton |
| Thomas Worthington | age 36 | Dataller | born: Westhoughton |
| Harry Wyper | age 21 | Collier | born: Hamsterley, Durham |
| Thomas Yates | age 30 | Drawer | born: Westhoughton |